C000134398

Outside Noise

ALESHA D. FITZGERALD

Outside Noise

© 2022 Alesha Fitzgerald

All rights reserved. No part of this publication may be reproduced, distributed, or transmitted in any form or by any means, including photocopying, recording, or other electronic or mechanical methods, without the prior written permission of the publisher, except in the case of brief quotations embodied in critical reviews and certain other non-commercial uses permitted by copyright law.

ISBN 978-1-66784-132-8

eBook ISBN 978-1-66784-133-5

FOREWORD: LIEUTENANT NICOLE REAVES

I have been afforded this great opportunity of writing the foreword for this book "Distracted" Outside Noise. My life as well as all of ours has been one distraction after another. I recall some of my distractions going back to my early years, but I will start around the time when I was about 8 years old. I suffered from being bullied accompanied with racism because I was apart of one of the first black families to move to the suburbs where there was nothing but all white families in the late 70's. That distraction was to keep me from concentrating on doing what needed to be done successful then, and later in life.

It wasn't until later in life that I realized that all the things that have ever happened to me that I didn't like were only meant to distract me long enough to stop focusing on my blessings and being grateful for what God had already given me. At the same time, possess the faith needed to know that God had already given it all to me, even before I would ask. The only time I would forget these things is when I succumbed to a distraction. Through the years, I've learned to be grateful for all things because there's always someone else out there that's worse off than you. I learned to live in the moment physically and spiritually but stay focused on the future. This was the cure to killing any outside noise that would occur.

In my adult years, the distractions that I endured was related to controlling all aspects of life in an extremely small manner. This was done by putting my focus on God first and all else fell into place in every and all situations in life.

When I first experienced love and a broken heart, there was a hole left in my soul. This was a huge distraction to every relationship that followed. It wasn't until I sought out God that HE healed the hole in my soul and my broken heart when I put HIM first. It took time and patience with

God, just as HE was with me, while staying focused on HIM, "GOD". The same was true when I got married. I learned that I shouldn't be distracted, and not to get caught up on every little thing. It is not the distraction that's important, but what is important, is loving your spouse the way you want to be loved.

As far as parenting goes, try not to focus on the distractions. Your job as a parent is to simply love your child and that's it. God gives us our children and if we give our children back to God, there is honor and reciprocity from God.

Those of us that worry are simply distracted and focusing on the outside noise, just like the enemy wants us to do, but by focusing on God first with faith, it abolishes the outside noise. For me, forgiveness has been the key to opening the flood of blessings from God, no matter how deep the scars, forgive yourself and others.

For those who may ask what makes me qualified to speak on these things, outside of my life experiences, I have my Associate's in Communications, my Bachelor's degree in Sociology, a Master's in Criminal Justice, and three years of graduate studies in Psychology. I have given my life to God and since then HE continues to bless me. When I met the author of this book, there was an immediate spiritual connection. God used both of us to bless one another. She is my spiritual sister, and I am so grateful to have her in my life. This book can apply to anyone's life because we all have the outside noise of distractions. Much love to my spiritual sister for writing this much needed guide that combines both our natural and spiritual lives.

Love always,

Lieutenant Nicole Reaves

Thank You's:

To my besties and sister friends: Ana, Crystal A., Crystal C., and my siblings who allow me to live in a rose-colored creative bubble and give me permission to tell them my dreams and goals for me and them and the help in building me up with great business ideas and life flowing wisdom, you were given to me by God! Love you more than you will ever know!

To: My Gorgeous! Thank you for your shoulder when I cry and your chest when I need comfort and your smile just to tell me hi! I love the life God is allowing us to create together! I Love you past who we are and pray for who God makes us into!

To my girls: (Dasia, Markayla, Aaliyah, Nakia, and Andrea): I've tried to walk through the fire so you won't feel the heat as an adult, I pray y'all remain fireproof and live the greatest life you can without stumbling on distractions! Pray first, pray through it, and pray consistently. God hears every word you say, make Him proud. I Love you all individually, unconditionally, and too much!

To our son: (Lil King) I cried for the relationship that didn't manifest, but one day it will beautiful boy!

To My Spiritual Sister Nicole: Thank you for imparting into me and my husband, reminding me what faith is, reminding me what real love is, believing in me, bleeding to heal me, pushing me to better, encouraging fasting and accountability, I love your wisdom and transparency so much!

To My Spiritual Brother Carlyle C. (KnGz): Thank you for support, poetry, and biblical balance! Your wisdom is worth so much more than money. It has pulled me from dark places many times unbeknownst to you, thank you for allowing your spirit to talk!

To my grandson: Your birth became my catalyst to start creating generational wealth, finish school, and achieve dream goals. We will push you to do the same in love. You're the beginning of another legacy, walk and believe in it. Love you too much!

CHAPTER 1.

Distracted in childhood:

Being bullied can cause scars which can spill over into adulthood.

This will cause one to be closed off, mean, and not willing to be vulnerable to anyone for help or just plain old teamwork! Being bullied is traumatic and can also cause stunted growth and be a distraction from living a full life of abundance in all areas. Two of my daughters were bullied in middle school and still deal with thinking someone is trying to be rude or being mean. They also stick up for people if they feel the individual is being bullied. Our second youngest almost got kicked out of school for taking up for a friend who was being bullied. Forgive everyone everything including yourself. You may feel guilty for not sticking up for yourself or running "what if" scenarios in your head. Let it go. It's a distraction! It's taking up too much space in your thought process! Use that time and those thoughts for entrepreneurship! The best revenge is being successful! Forgiving yourself will make you feel so much better! I had the hardest time forgiving myself for things that weren't even in my control for years! The sheer thought of those situations would cause me to cry each time I thought of it! But God delivered me from the "pseudo-control" I had. He also removed the shame and guilt associated with being a teen mom and being human period. I now love myself as a human and forgive myself daily!

Father God I pray that we recognize past hurts, call out current bullying tactics, even if it's us against ourselves, and forgive them to make our futures and others better. Amen!

CHAPTER 2.

Distracted as an adolescent:
This is the period where friends have a huge impact on your life.

Birds of a feather flock together rings true in this age gap. Friends start bad habits together, cross milestones together. My friend had her son three months after I had my fourth daughter. We lost our virginity within months of each other. I was always getting her into trouble in high school! I was a naughty friend to hang around because I was angry and didn't care about much. Monitor who you call a friend, monitor how their home life is, monitor what they say about their family, monitor what their hobbies are, what they spend their time on and with whom. I think friends are phenomenal when they are a great choice. They are free therapy if you feel vulnerable enough to allow them to be, they are great inspiration, encouragement, and motivation! Always pray for your friends. You never know when they are fighting silent battles that only God knows about. Proverbs 18:24 NIV says "One who has unreliable friends soon comes to ruin, but there is a friend who sticks closer than a brother" you will have fair weather friends, you will have some friends for a season, and some for a lifetime that will be there during bad relationships, jobs, homes, children, and financial losses and wins. Love them all regardless of their purpose and Thank God for each one! Always celebrate each other! Be encouraging to each other!

Father God, I pray you send us great friends that will feed each season that we are in. I pray that we recognize when to let friends go whose season is complete and cherish the lifetime friendships. May we also know how to listen, encourage, and be a great friend. Amen!

CHAPTER 3.

Distracted as an adult:
The idea of being a perfect parent made my 20s stressful!

My expectations were that I wanted to be a better mother and person. I had a people pleasing demeanor and was passive aggressive at home because I was tired from helping everyone else and not leaving anytime or forgiveness for myself. "Me time" was never a part of my schedule during that time. I started nursing school at 23 when my daughters were 2,3,4 and 6 years old. So I had two at home and two in school, their dad was on drugs or in jail during this period. I had a high level of anxiety wanting them to be safe at school and wanting them to be better than me and wanting to elevate where I was at in order to provider better for them. We were living in subsidized housing in the middle of the city of Milwaukee. One day my oldest came home and said some little boy punched my 4-year-old in the stomach and she couldn't get to her and there was no teacher around! Words couldn't express how angry I was, and I talked to the teacher about it and told them to let her be near her sister and why wasn't there a teacher outside to watch 4-year-old children! They didn't go back the following year! They had put my daughters on the wrong bus also. I started transporting them myself! I was super involved, super overprotective and anxious all the time! It was horrible. But I had a great support system in their grandma who had her own daycare and my family helped a lot.

I was second guessing myself constantly and wanting them to be happy and not write books on me when they got older about how horrible I was! (One of my biggest fears!) but I was humble enough to learn better parenting techniques from my friends and their grandmother, and to talk more, yell less or not at all. Punish less, speak way more! Be an example and monitor everything they say, do, and who they are exposed to. You can't control everything, but you can talk about anything to help them through it all. Pray often as a parent! Encourage them constantly! Love on them every chance you get, time goes by so fast! You blink and they're in puberty and hate affection, blink again they are adults! Build them up so that they will know that with God they can become anything they want to become!

Heavenly Father, thank you for entrusting us with your children! Help and guide us to impart into our children what You want! Remind us to pray for them, encourage them, and be transparent with them to help them be better. Father God, you said for us to raise up a child in the way that he should go, and he will never depart from it. (Proverbs 22:6 NIV) Thank you Lord that they will know you, in Jesus' name, Amen!

CHAPTER 4.

Distracted in love

*The biggest distraction for me in love
has been a broken heart from disloyalty.*

Loving others harder than I loved my own self. The Bible tells us to protect our heart (Proverbs 4:23) but I didn't get that memo until much later, so I walked around broken and unsealed with a lot of emotional baggage. So, when Erykah Badu wrote Bag Lady I understood and felt like the poster child for the song! Healing took time, but I wasn't allowing myself to heal in an empty bed. Which in turn cost me more scars, when I realized what was wrong, I allowed myself to be alone and break, I needed the potter to mend and mold my cracked porcelain pieces. (Isaiah 64:8) He created me, so I had to go back to HIM for the healing. I also had to trust Him, not me. I messed up so many times and made so many mistakes (bad thinking, not forgiving me for being human) that I second guessed everything I did before I did it. Which caused me to be stuck and not progressing in any area because I didn't trust me anymore.

Being patient with the process of healing can be a distraction if you're impatient. Be patient and allow the grace of God to heal you as well. New mercies every day He gives us (Lamentations 3:22-23), so we must give that same mercy to ourselves and others. You can't rewrite history, but you can learn from it and help someone else to not walk in it. Therefore sharing our experiences or testimonies are so important to educating the next generation.

Impatience is a distraction: thinking you know what time things should happen and not trusting God's will and HIS timing. Isaiah 55:8 NIV "For my thoughts are not your thoughts, neither are your ways my ways."

He is omnipresent, omnipotent, and omniscient, HE already knows how it will work out and how it will get done, and who to use to help you! I raised 4 daughters as a single mom and went to nursing school and worked at Walmart part time when they were 2,3,4, and 6. When I graduated, they were 10, 8, 7, and 6. God allowed me to get a place in low-income housing while going to school and kept us safe the entire time! There was gambling going on in front of the Section 8 housing, I seen someone get robbed of his shoes one night in the middle of the sidewalk that connected a section of the project homes. I was too distracted to thank Him for it, worrying about gas money, and writing papers, and food! We still made it without going hungry and without being evicted. Please know that "…with God All Things Are Possible!" (Matthew 19:26 NIV)

Father God, I thank you for the opportunities to love and forgive myself and my loved ones. Thank you for making my life possible even when I doubted. I pray my life is an example to others and they start believing that YOU can and Will in their life, just as you did in mine! In Jesus name, Amen!

CHAPTER 5.

Distracted in marriage:
Marriage is a bond of friendship between two people with
GOD and love as the glue that holds it.
"Keywords here is GOD and friendship. GOD is LOVE

When done correctly marriage is a beautiful example to others letting them know that they can also succeed at it. It takes prayer, communication, friendship, and forgiveness! My marriage shows me areas that I still am selfish in, areas where I need to improve my communication in, and where I need to pray/strengthen/motivate my husband at. You are a team with interchangeable roles. You may be a coach on a day where they have an important meeting, or their cheerleader when they are feeling down. You become responsible for them. I pray daily that God gives me His strength to love all my loved ones with His heart not mine. That's too much for my heart. But David said, "Create in me a clean heart and renew in me a right spirit". (Psalms 51:10 KJV) You can't love selfishly in a marriage or as a parent! Love requires you to not think about you. It's putting your heart out there for definite heartbreak if you have expectations. One of my favorite sayings is forgive everyone everything and love everyone past yourself! I'm not saying marriage is easy, it takes God and work. It's a responsibility that you are taking on to working even on days when you want to quit and a mile or so past that! "Be not weary in well doing!" (Galatians 6:9) There are days where you feel like you are being taken advantage of, unappreciated, and even unloved. The daily distractions of work stress, finances, previous relationship trash, family dynamics and stress pulling on the marriage, unspoken expectations of each other, internal conversations and conflicts that go unspoken. Unspoken internal "failures" (perception). Parental challenges and disagreements. Different goals for children, different parenting styles. Temptations, tempers, and less time spent together. Pray! Consistently pray!

Tell God first in prayer, and then your spouse so that they can validate you. If you hold it, there will be passive anger just stuffed down and secret regrets, please take it from me and communicate! In this day and age of social media and detached communication, write an old-fashioned letter if you want them to hear your heart! Be vulnerable, it's ok, God will heal each crack in your heart! He Did it for me! Do date nights, flirt, go to church together, cook for them, pray for them, and encourage them. Love them how you want to be loved and beyond. I love my husband the way I want God to love me, but I know God loves me way more! God will bless your obedience and sacrifice!

Father God Thank you for sustaining marriages in this season of a pandemic. During this time may all marriages be brought closer together, have more intimate and healing conversations, and renew the friendship that will make a lasting marriage. For we know marriages represent how Jesus loves the church. May all marriages be examples of your love in Jesus' name, Amen!

CHAPTER 6.

Distracted parenting:
Lord Help me to pay attention!

When I learned of me becoming a mom for the first time, I experienced a sense of fear and failure at the same time because I was 16, a junior in high school, and not at all ready! Her first kicks were reassuring that we will be just fine, and we were great! She is now 25 and a mother to her only child! As a parent I wanted to give them everything, but you can't until one is ready or it will be mismanaged! I gave my oldest a car I got off the showroom floor, Praise God, but within a few months, she had a friend who jumped on the hood to dance and dented it in and broke an air filter and hose underneath the hood! $400 worth of damage! I was too mad at her mismanagement, but I should have assessed her level of maturity before giving her the car. Most children are the prodigal son or the brother! Most parents are the king, ready to run out and meet their baby because they came back to us! And we put them back in their same position! Put the robe and ring back on them and encourage them! Allow them to tell you their experience, (everyone has a different perception) and encourage them towards better! Love on them always! Correct them in love, tell them often how proud you are and that they are exactly where God wants them and that they need to also be patient with where God has them and where HE is taking them. Help them to achieve their dreams, for they are an extension of you. Forgive their mistakes, they are already beating their own selves up, no reason to add salt to it, pour the water of Gods water on it to show them loving kindness. They will thank you for it. I learned the most about God's patient unconditional love, grace, and mercy through parenthood. Enjoy the journey!

Heavenly Father, thank you for blessing our lives with children and trusting us by giving us one of your children, and to be the first example of your love. Please give us the opportunity to be tuned into our children, whether biological or love connected. May we be the place that they will be comfortable enough to be vulnerable with. May we point them back to you, pray with them and for them. In Jesus' name, Amen!

CHAPTER 7.

Distracted driving:
Metaphorically about life

U-Turns: when you're going one way and you get turned around. Like making a horrible mistake and rerouting yourself to have a favorable outcome. In nursing school, I failed a whole semester because I didn't trust my intuition/my holy spirit that told me to stay out that semester. I was a semester ahead because of summer school, but I wanted to graduate early. Well, I failed and got kicked out of school. I got accepted back in and graduated with my best friends. God's timing is always right, obedience to your spirit will make the tests shorter and blessings come quicker!

Slow drivers: When you must be somewhere at a certain time, and you end up behind a slow driver. Oh, my goodness, this would drive me nuts when I was younger. It was also a habit of mine to be later all the time. I had to get sick and tired of rushing and being anxious about being late. I learned to wake up early enough to get my thoughts together, to be grateful for waking up, and prepare my clothes and lunch the night before.

I would thank God each time I go around that slow driver and there's an accident ahead that could've easily been me! God will turn your mistakes into messages.

Speeding: When you think you're going at a good speed and you will get somewhere on time when its just spurts of going fast then you end up the same place as the car you passed up.... distraction... drive the speed limit and get there safely. There are too many car crashes each year for mistakes that can be avoided. Be cautious and aware when driving. Cars are a tool to be used to transport you safely, use it safely so that it may continue to serve you for a long time.

Being cut off: One of my biggest pet peeves when someone jumps in front of you and then slows down, Help Me Lord!!! But it's a distraction, takes your focus away from your current goal... whether it's a collection when you're fixing your credit or an unpaid ticket driving your car insurance up... ignore it and go around it, and thank God for not allowing them to hit you on your road to success.

Fast lanes: the best moments in your life fly by, enjoy it! Ride in it as long as you can doing the speed limit! Create the life that will make you feel like this always! I love going to Los Angeles where they have the fast lane that goes for miles upon miles! Sometimes it continues to flow when the other 6 lanes are backed up. Enjoy a life that will continue to produce when others are in a rut. Not saying you are to gloat, always be humble, but create a life that you want to wake up to and continue to smile about each day. Being in awe about how God is blessing you!

Red lights: Stop, don't coast through them. Obey the laws of the land. Your paused for a reason, reflect in this space and redirect your focus if you need to. A lot of my greatest Aha moments have been at a pause in my life. We all need a pause in our lives, consider it a rest break where you plot your next direction.

Yellow lights: These caution lights are for your protection. Pump your breaks to slow down or if you know you can safely make it, do so. But this is quick thinking moments. You know where you're going, so think fast. All the research better be done by now during this opportunity.

Green lights: Go! Make sure the path is clear and go! Be clear, focused, goal oriented and ignoring all distractions! This is your moment! Go determined, goal oriented, and being mindful about your future.

Exit lanes: know when your exit is... when is the last straw, when it has become too uncomfortable and you're too unhappy, time to exit! God sometimes makes us uncomfortable when it's time for us to go up another level. You will know also but will still try and stay at that job because you don't want to make new friends or you like your routine... no excuses! Put your signal on and get off easy street! Challenge yourself! Push yourself to greatness!

Father God I pray that we will know where you are calling us to be. Let us be so in tuned to your voice that we will understand when you are calling us to greater and that we will be obedient in listening to that prompting. We give you permission to make us uncomfortable. In Jesus name, Amen!

CHAPTER 8.

Outside noise of people:
Respond to me right!

I would get distracted by people because they weren't responding the way I expected them to respond! Nonsense, right? I can't control people. But I thought I could make and keep them happy if I did things for them. But I was totally unhappy if their reactions weren't what I expected. It took me a long time to release myself from that type of thinking! It's dangerous to take on the responsibility of someone's happiness. What if they are going through something that has nothing to do with you? I would attempt to make my boyfriend happy, and he may have been dwelling on something negative that happened to him as a child. I can't go back and fix that! He maybe so scarred that I can't even make him smile at that moment. What could happen is a prayer and a conversation about forgiveness. That takes the responsibility off me and points him to a God who can actually help heal it. I had to walk my daughters up to the casket of their father. When I say I felt helpless, broken, and scared is just the beginning of the onslaught of emotions that I felt. I literally realized this is something I can't fix in no way at all. My prayers went deeper, they had to include my daughters' minds and broken hearts! Before I felt like maybe it was too surface, too ritualistic, too "churchy", it wasn't genuine enough and felt rehearsed! But God! I was now on my face; Lord help our daughters! (He gave/trusted them to me to raise them, but they are His). Prayer was my weapon to combat anxiety, fear, worry, depression! My best friend had passed 6 months prior to this, I now had a problem sleeping without crying. God help me, please let me live to see them all graduate, now it's Lord, I thank you for everyday! Seek Him first, love people but love you enough to know your boundaries and lead people back to Jesus!

Don't allow anyone to ruin you, allow God to build you."

Don't allow anyone to ruin your self-confidence or self-worth, that's giving them too much power.

Some people will try and put their fears into you! Saying what they would do if they were you, or what you should and shouldn't do. People were waiting on me to fail when I started college. Or waiting for me to quit because it was "too hard". Block the negative and put in your mind where you see you at! Your vision of your life is powerful! See yourself winning! See yourself walking across that stage accepting your diploma! See your bank account with multiple zeros! See yourself with the keys in your hand to your new house in the neighborhood you want to live in! You're not a sell out if you want to live in a better neighborhood! You want to be safe! It's our goal to raise our children and grandchildren in a neighborhood of better so they can be used to seeing it and not expect anything of a lower standard. The Prodigal Son knew he was better than a pig pen! (Luke 15:17). You can have greater! Believe it! We can always think better of someone else's situation than our own, believe in better for you also! See it solved in your favor!

I desired for my children to do great! But I had to show them! I speak into their lives that they will be successful, and they will prosper and do great things in life! God is their guide! Period!

Focused Life: Ephesians 3:20 NLT *"Now all glory to God, who is able, through his mighty power at work within us, to accomplish infinitely more than we might ask or think"* This promise right here is amazing! God has put me in the presence of millionaires to guide and educate me into the real estate business. HE has placed people in my life that encourage and push me to be a level better when I'm still happy with the last level! This worship life will have you joyous and thinking sunshine and marigold thoughts which is necessary when you're the friend or family member that must go into prayer for another person. I don't allow unforgiveness, impatience, anger, selfishness, money, worry, or anything else to keep me from gratitude and praying for another. I'm sure I am living on my ancestors and grandmother's prayers. I not only owe it to God for being gracious and merciful but also our ancestors whose scarred backs and hands helped to bring us to this point. I couldn't have gone to college if it wasn't for them marching and voting for integrated schools. I honored my grandmother by becoming a nurse and taking care of all people in an unbiased manner. My mother's mother is who would take me with her as an in-home health aide and I watched her take care of Oma, an elderly German lady who I learned how to speak German in middle school just so I can communicate with her in her language. I would help my grandmother with her bed bath and put clean clothes on her on weekends. It wasn't child labor, it was a teaching experience that helped me to know that caring for others came naturally to me, and I should be a nurse, even though I wanted to be a teacher. God granted me my heart's desire of being a teacher on 2 occasions, as a psychiatric nurse teaching in an outpatient setting, and as a clinical instructor for LPN students, encouraging willing students to be great nurses who serve their patients wholeheartedly. God wants a willing heart to worship Him without distractions, He tells us in Matthew 6:33 KJV *"But seek Ye first the kingdom of God; and all these things shall be added unto you."* I want all that God has for me! Not only that but I want His guidance, comfort, and peace above all things, so I must seek Him. I've done everything else, sex didn't help, alcohol didn't help, education, money, people, none of it empowered me like obedience, worship, prayer, and gratitude does. A good prayer will make you wake up smiling when it's raining! And I thought for sure I had seasonal affective disorder. Not at all, I was just depressed, and in my opinion, disconnected from God. HE can't guide you if you're not talking to HIM. How can your parent help you if you don't talk to them or have any kind of relationship with them? They love you regardless but will spoil you when connected. Psalm 84:11 NLT *"For the Lord is our sun and shield. He gives us grace and glory. The Lord will withhold no good thing from those who do what is right.* "And when you talk to Him in prayer He will guide you in righteousness, He will give you good ideas for businesses and books. HE gave me this idea for this book I am writing at the moment. No good thing will HE withhold. (Psalms 84:11b NIV) My life has been going up steadily since I started following God, it takes focus and obedience. But I want to be an example for my daughters like my grandmother was for me. I desire to do right! This life is awesome, I love seeing my prayers get answered fast! God giving me the desires of my heart! I wouldn't go back!

Heavenly Father, may we always desire to be close to you so that you may guide, heal, help, and teach us. Help us to know you in a greater way instead of trying to seek people's approval. May your word show us something new each time we read to seek you, In Jesus name, Amen!

CHAPTER 9.

Distracted by worry:
"It keeps running through my head"

"Mark 8:36 *For what shall it profit a man if he gains
the world and loses his soul."*

Worrying, which is a distraction, profited me nothing! I lost time worrying about bills, raising my daughters, work, all I really did was get sick. My stomach and head hurt frequently when I stressed out, I smoked cigarettes for over 15 years. I would even worry about what my patients would think if they knew I smoked as a nurse. I felt like a hypocrite, pushing preventative medicine, but hurting myself with all the chemicals in the cigarettes that were supposed to help with the stress, but only caused me to worry about getting chronic obstructive pulmonary disease or lung cancer. Then I would pray because I had no sick time and then back to worrying about who will have to raise the girls if I did get sick! Makes me tired just thinking about all those negative thoughts now!

But when I prayed, and believed things changed, my perspective changed! I quit smoking shortly after their father died. I felt so selfish at the time wanting to smoke when I was the only parent that they had left. I didn't want to get older and be on oxygen and dependent on one of them to take care of me because I chose to not change. That was so unfair but Thank God I quit. I changed my mind, prayed and got help with quitting. You have the power to change your mind and God will do the rest and make it smoother not easier. Every day I chose to not smoke, took the medication to quit, and walked in the freedom from that addiction! " Philippians 4:8 NIV ".... *finally, brothers and sisters, whatever is true, whatever is noble, whatever is right, whatever is pure, whatever is lovely, whatever is admirable-if anything is excellent or praiseworthy – think about such things."* What Apostle Paul is saying is for us to think about the positive to be positive. The more positive you put in, the more positive will come out. When I realized how much time I spent worrying and being anxious about nothing, my daughters were adults. It was all for naught!

Distracted thinking cost me memories and I allowed it!

Now, I enjoy every moment God gives me. I barely argue with my husband, I find a reason to smile and laugh with him again. Life is too short to be angry or not speak. God requires for us to love everyone the way HE loves us! As hard as it sounds, HE equips us to do it!

Believe me I have been spit on, kicked, thrown out of a house with small children, punched, glass broken out in my face, sprayed with bug spray, cussed out, hot water thrown on me in minus 13 degree weather 7 months pregnant and then stomped for leaving, chased by someone with a gun, raped, present in a burglary, on W-2, broke, borrowing money for food, borrowing food stamps from friends, visiting a baby daddy in prison, buried loved ones, money stolen by drug addicts, cheated on, lied on, manipulated by loved ones, car stolen, abandoned, and abused mentally. I forgave them all, and myself for allowing it. God has restored everything that was stolen and healed what was broken!

Father God, I thank you for forgiveness. I thank you that I can and have forgiven and that you have and continue to forgive me. I am human will never be perfect, and I am thankful for your new grace and mercy daily! Please remind me to forgive me consistently as well. I love you Lord, in Jesus' name, Amen!

CHAPTER 10.

Unforgiveness is another distraction!
"Every time I think about it, I just get mad all over again!"

My mom was diagnosed with stage 3 lymphoma that was on her stomach, esophagus, and pancreas. Prior to this she had pneumonia, had fallen on 4 separate occasions, and I moved her in with our family. During this time also I had started a new job, started my second semester of graduate school, and was dealing with empty nest syndrome. Stress and depression was my new normal and I kept telling myself that *"....To whom much is given, much is required"* (Luke 12:48B) I am a nurse so it was "naturally" expected of me to help my mom, but I still had unforgiveness issues and was hard hearted towards her. My answers would be short, phone calls would be at a minimum. I was just disappointed! Yet another distraction! My expectations of what a parent is, was the reason that I was disappointed. But God allowed me to think about how it took her mistakes to help me be a better parent. I may have been a statistic as a teen mom, but none of my daughters were! They all graduated high school, yet only my brother actually did, myself and my other siblings all earned our GED. One brother accomplished this in prison, which I blamed her for as well, but I needed to forgive her.

I started thinking, who am I to dictate how someone parents! How dare I judge what and how she parented. She only did what she knew to do, what she could do, and used what she had to raise us. My expectations was Claire Huxtable from The Cosby Show. That wasn't reality though, with God and a changed mind I turned it around for my 4 daughters with the assistance of their grandmother who is still one of my favorite people! She is filled with loving kindness and gentle, and patient, and hilarious! God gave me her as an example of HIS unconditional love. I was open, vulnerable, and willing to learn from her, and she didn't mind pouring into me and being a selfless example. She became my spiritual mother and assisted me in parenting my daughters. God will send you help to be great!

Realizing that I must be an example of how I want my daughters to treat me, and regardless everyone makes mistakes even when you don't know the mistakes you've made! When I worked at a private psychiatric hospital, I learned some people have trigger words that others won't know unless they are told. So, if you're in a conversation with someone and you say it "mistakenly" who's wrong? Forgiveness is a must for complete healing! My mom has since moved out, I continue to help and honor her. We communicate just fine, and she has been cancer free for 3 years! Prayer works y'all!

Father God Thank you for help! Thank you for urging us to be better through the examples of others. Thank you for trusting us to serve and be an example to others as well. Thank you for helping me to pass the test of forgiveness and learning from other's mistakes. In Jesus name, Amen!

CHAPTER 11.

Distracted by your self-perception
"I look so fat! I am so dumb!"

The outside noise can be internal. One becomes their own enemy. (In a me)(en e my) Rehearsing lines of brokenness, disrespect, defeat, failure, can't, wonts, poverty, unworthiness, unfaithfulness, and ugliness! I know it's not just me who thought this way! When bad things happened it further confirmed these thoughts. I second guessed every decision! I didn't trust myself not to mess up! I knew if I fell, my daughters would fall with me, and I couldn't handle dropping them more than I already had. Being an unwed, uneducated, teen mom made me feel like an utter, and unprepared failure. But God! I now believe and know that *"All things work out for the good of those that love Him..."* (Romans 8:28) and that *"I was made in the image and likeness of God"* (Genesis 1:26), so thinking negatively about me was indeed talking about God! I had to dismiss those thoughts! Each time I would "change my mind", think something better! Think about where I wanted to go on my next trip, dream about what I wanted my life to look like. I knew if I could defeat this spirit of low self-esteem, I could pull out my daughters if they crossed this same path! A lot of what we go through is for us to help someone else! I am unselfish enough to get through it and look for someone to help through. I am transparent about my life if someone were to ask. I'm not the type to be on social media documenting my every move. That's a distraction and I don't like media platforms in that manner. I appreciate it for the marketing purposes. But like anything else, use it for what it's for. Allow God to be your diary, not Facebook, Instagram, or Twitter!

I know me now and I know what works to help me be more productive. Don't allow your perceptions to make you feel as if you don't matter! You light up someone's world when you walk in, someone is happy when you call, whether they act like it or not! Someone enjoys your smile! There will never be another you! Be your biggest cheerleader at all times!!!!!

Heavenly Father, forgive me for thinking negative of what You created and called a masterpiece. Thank you for teaching me that You made me in Your image and in Your likeness. I am thankful for what you have given me. May I treat and protect what you have given me in a great manner that you are proud of. In Jesus name, Amen!

CHAPTER 12.

Distracted by emotions:
No emotional decisions!

When you're feeling angry or sad, don't make any decisions at that moment. Just ride out the feeling while telling yourself I can get through this, I can still overcome this, I can and will win regardless of what it looks like! My latter will be greater! I love my life, it's better than I've ever could've dreamed, and I am a dreamer!!!! But I would make emotional decisions and later regret it. When you allow your emotions to delegate where you're headed, you will go in circles! For example, getting mad and breaking up with someone instead of being vulnerable enough to say what hurt my feelings. Or quitting a job prior to securing another position. Think all decisions through completely, including the future aspects of the decision. Have peace about the decision before finalizing, meaning if you keep second guessing the decision, it's probably not the right one if it's been over 24 hours.

What if you knew that holding on making that extra effort would impact your children's children well-being? Would you do it? Well, in actuality it does. **"No man is an island unto himself"** means that everything you do impacts someone else! A huge responsibility when you think about it! Rosa Park's decision totally impacted everyone as did Dr. Martin Luther King Jr, Malcolm X, Mahatma Ghandi, Mother Theresa, etc.

My grandmother's decision to move to Milwaukee impacted where I would live and raise my children. Every decision you make affects someone else. When I finally realized this principle, I started overthinking everything! But I didn't trust myself also which I have since corrected!

But please pray first and think about the consequences of all the choices before making a final decision.

Father God Thank you for a sound mind, peace, and the ability to pray knowing that You hear me! Thank you that your word is a lamp unto my feet and a light onto my path. May we always seek you before making a decision. In Jesus name, Amen!

CHAPTER 13.

Distracted Communication:
You ever had a conversation that went south
because of outside noise?

Like you're talking to someone and they are not paying attention or you want their full face towards you and their empathy but they are playing a game (my hubby) and not giving you a 100% of their attention.

Intentional listening! Focused listening! Being vulnerable to the conversation and the person.

Being in the present moment to really hear what the person is saying, not just listening enough to answer them, but hearing even the subtle inflections in their voice. My husband says ok in a way that means he's not going to repeat himself if he feels someone isn't listening, and I have to restate what he said so he knows I heard him. This is also how you build trust in any relationship. My husband won my heart because he knows me, because he listens even when I think he hasn't. He knows from the non-verbal cues when I'm going to cry. Several times he has just stood there and as soon as I turn to him, he opens his arms and gives me his shoulder and holds me. That's understanding that took listening, paying attention, and time to cultivate.

As a parent, your children will rely on you taking time to step outside of your own head to help them with what's going on in theirs. You may not have it all together, but you can help them by listening first, then work it out together. Texting, emails, and social media has made face to face conversation harder than it used to be. Reading body language will soon be obsolete. Looking into one's eyes is not commonplace for some; it will soon be a thing only for job interviews. I'm not an eye contact person as it is, it feels too intimate, but I understand that eye contact is needed at times. James 1:9 NKJV "...*be quick to listen and slow to speak.*" It's a way of saying seek first to understand before trying to be understood. It keeps us from being selfish and makes us focus on our loved ones. It also gives one an opportunity to teach our children a different point of view or correct their thinking if needed. Children will think they are correct in what they do also. Parenting involves correction and repeating values, morals, and modeling the behavior you expect of them.

Father God, teach us to be listeners, first to your word, then attuned to what someone is saying, desiring to understand first and then to be understood. In Jesus name, Amen!

CHAPTER 14.

Distracted goals
Distractions will keep you from reaching your goals!

For example, if you're distracted by your boyfriend thinking that he's cheating, you won't be able to focus on the dreams you've seen. God gives us dreams to keep us motivated until HE gives them to us! I was distracted in a relationship for 4 years! He was really cheating but I kept thinking "but I didn't catch him" but every time we broke up I got blessed! But I would then go right back. It had become a cycle of distracted destruction in my life. I lost almost everything and when I was finally done. I got everything back double! I met someone who would later become my best friend a few months later. We went slow because I couldn't trust my decisions, was broken, and distrustful. That 4-year distracted cycle taught me to forgo sex. That is in and of itself a serious distraction! It's a temporary bliss that hides the identity of a person. It makes everything they do cute! Later on you will wonder why you didn't realize that a certain action is annoying! (i.e. what was I thinking!) Be a friend first, pray together and for each other. Know what their goals are, and if their goals are consistent with where you are also going.

Advice: Continually reach for your goals, make new goals to reach when you accomplish past goals, don't allow any distractions to keep you from forward movement, be patient in the process. Pray through it all!

Father God, help us to recognize all distractions so that we may continue to move forward and not be stuck in the distraction. May we continue to reference your word for our life. In Jesus name, Amen!

Distraction Tips:

1. Mind Your Own Business. When you mind your own business, you're not stooping down finding dirt and picking that dirt up to sling it back to the haters who throw it first. People who mind their OWN business are literally minding their Business! What it looks like financially, the sustainability of the product, what employees they want, the way the company flows, the mission, vision, and values are! Mentally projecting where they want to see their company in 2, 5, and 10 years, who their target audience is, how they should market. Don't stop your positive future driven thoughts to address someone bending down in your past and slinging it. You know what your past was, keep driving forward towards your goals, no reason to be distracted by what you drove past already!

2. Distractions can keep us from being aware of others needs or issues that we may be able to assist them with. Whether it's a listening ear, a word of encouragement, finances, or a prayer. We are our brother's/sister's keeper.

3. If you're going to be distracted, be distracted by your goals, by helping someone else, by thinking about your next steps to financial success, or entrepreneurship ideas. Be distracted about who needs prayer, be distracted by who you need to bless.

4. Address the distraction: is it emotional? Calm down before making a decision.

5. Refocus your attention back to the goal/task needed to be completed.

6. Don't look back at it once your put it down. God can't keep saving you from what you keep picking back up.

7. Don't allow "distractions" during me time. This is the time for you to refuel in order to be better for your loved ones.

8. Encourage yourself during the distraction. You're still human, you need the positive feedback to fuel the hope in your soul. Have friends also that will cheer you on and vice versa.

9. Have mentors that you look up to that are on the level you are aiming for, and they are "pushing" you to get there also!

10. Don't stay stagnant, always go to the next level.

11. Read, Read, Read! You will never be the smartest person, but you can try one book/article/blog at a time!

12. Help someone else when you are going through, their problem will clarify yours, or make you grateful for your own.

ENCOURAGING SCRIPTURES FOR DEFEATING DISTRACTIONS

1 Thessalonians 5:13 NIV: Live in Peace with One Another

Psalms 27: 13-14 NIV: I remain confident in this: that I will see the goodness of the Lord in the land of the living. Wait for the Lord; be strong take heart and wait for the Lord!

Psalms 27:4 NIV: One thing that I ask of the Lord, That I may dwell in the house of the Lord all the days of my life.

Psalms 23:6 NIV: Surely your goodness and mercy shall follow me all of my days and I will dwell in the house of the Lord Forever.

Philippians 4: 4-9 NIV: Rejoice in the Lord Always. I will say it again, Rejoice. Let your gentleness be evident to all. The Lord is near. Don't be anxious for anything but in every situation by prayer and petition with thanksgiving, present your requests to God. And the peace of God which transcends all understanding, will guard your heart and your minds in Christ Jesus. Finally, brothers and sisters, whatever is right, whatever is pure, whatever is lovely, whatever is admirable-if anything is excellent or praiseworthy – think about such things. Whatever you have learned or received or heard from me or seen in me-put into practice. And the God of peace will be with you.

SOMETIMES

With Good The Seed Sewn

Nothing is Ever Grown

Dreams Forgotten Long often are abandoned for Newer

Songs

So, where does that Good Seed go?

For There are Many…

Beneath dry soils they Lay

Nestled perfectly, they wait

For a few drops of The

Moisture…. on some Day.

Many Seeds come in Dreams

Some are Brought forth in

Schemes….

However so, they are planted as

"Viable Seed" in our Fertile

Souls.

The very power of our "Faith is the Moisture"
that will cause all of them to Grow.

KnGz 210914

FEAR

The fears distract and the years they pass

For nothing lives

Beyond a Man's thoughts without effort to

Give

Keep your feet moving

And be diligent not enamored by the dreamy glamour

Seek the realities now all dreams unrealized are fallacies spoken to the self

Casting aspersions, thus abandoned beautiful realities are left on the shelf

To focus is to Pray: May Jah's love deliver such unto thee according to all individuals power of

Faith… Trust and pray

We digress for rest from the stress we place upon our own chests…we forget, distracted again, years consumed….

Dreams Doomed.

It's improper etiquette to request a Bless from Heavens Best, yet neglect to Act:

Faith without works is inactivity…thus the

Diligent one prevails as the slothful one delays, self-distracts, and fails… and the only true failure. is the Failure to Try.

Do as we believe, stay Focused, don't self-deceive, or Dream in "Hokus-Pokus"…

Deliver us from evils of the distracted mind (it's human nature to dread and delay that we FEAR, and we self-soothe with our choice of distractions) & it's Manifest that we are So afraid to win the day.

Distraction is a form of Fear.

Fear is a Lack of Faith

Faith without works is Death

Death can occur multiple times in life we

Fail to live our Dreams.

KnGz!

7/5/21

THIS POETRY

This poetry right here is soul baring

Tearing off pieces of myself and exposing my heart
daring others to hurt it

It's soul worthy and this relationship with God makes me worth it

To receive what He shed for

Drop by drop draining His heart for us to return ours to Him

Dripping His life source each drop representing
a healing for all situations

It's not all peaches and cream rainbows and dreams

It's stretching, crying, and praying to get us to
the day of the future He plans

And the people who He prepared us to bleed for

Giving them a glimpse beyond the cuts scrapes and
scars to bare our heart to repair theirs

We are brought from a place that we can't stay in and
bought with a price, with no refund granted.

Elevation, determination, and motivation has to be a
continuous prayer daily to reach Him.

Don't be selfish expose yourself so that others may
pass it on to illuminate others

Learning from you the light source

To whom much is given much is required with Jesus
it was blood humility and selflessness

For us it's praising, praying, and a continuous need for Him

Knowing what we are called to be, He's worth it!

Amen!

Soul Deep 03/2017

CONCLUSION:

I hope you live your best life ignoring the distractions in this life. They will come and this book highlights what the distractions are and how to deal with them. Pray first, and a lot, increase your communication not only with your Creator but also have more encouraging talks with yourself, your family, and friends! Listen more than you speak, pray more when you want to complain! Allow yourself to freely be happy, have joy and a peace of mind. All of which will free your heart to love deeper and enjoy life before it gets away! Walk in all the blessings that are promised to you! Envision where you want your life to be and how it will look! Dream big enough that others will laugh when you tell them, until it happens for you, then you get to laugh!

Father God I love and adore you! I thank you for giving me an opportunity to teach again Lord! I pray you use me to reach many with all the glory belonging to you Lord! I pray all that reads this book will have an increase in their peace of mind, joy, happiness, and will develop better communication with you Lord and others, change their minds in the areas that You illuminate with this book, and retain these principles in their heart for focused living as an example to others. May God continually Bless you and everyone connected to you always In Jesus name, AMEN!

REFERENCES

Crawford, C. (KnGz) (2021, 14 September). *"Sometimes"*.

Crawford, C. (KnGz) (2021, 05 July). *"Fear"*.

Fitzgerald, A. (Soul Deep). (2017, March). *"This Poetry"*.

New International Version Bible. (2004-2021). Bible Hub. https://biblehub.org